GW00992164

Table of Contents

Introduction

The Labrador Retriever is one of the most loved and sought after dog breeds in the world. This characteristically gorgeous breed is recognized for its remarkable adaptability and extreme intellect. The Labrador Retriever is clever and gifted and capable of assuming countless different roles, including:

- Companion dog
- Family pet
- Herding dog
- Show dog
- Obedience dog
- Working dog
- Guide dog for the blind
- Hearing dog for the deaf
- Search and rescue dog
- Tracking dog
- Hunting dog
- TV actors

… And much more

The Labrador Retriever is branded by its superior intellect, great inquisitiveness, unlimited drive, adaptability and majestic good looks. These cunning dogs are extremely easy to train and will be enthusiastic to learn new tricks and means of pleasing their owners. This excitement and vigor begins at a very young age.

Nevertheless, as gifted and easy to train as they are, there will be times when a Labrador Retriever's owner may feel discouraged and impatient if they don't see quick or much success. You should know that this does sometimes happen. There are many reasons why this can happen. For instance, when your training techniques do not take into consideration what is essential to your specific dog and what makes him/her want to obey you the most.

Chapter 1: Is a Labrador Retriever Puppy/Dog a Good Fit For You?

As smart and attractive as Labrador Retrievers might be, it is essential to keep in mind that they are not the right fit for everyone. Because of their natural extraordinary intelligence and inquisitiveness, Labrador Retrievers require much mental stimulation in order to keep them from becoming bored.

Labrador Retrievers need lots of exercise. Taking your dog for walks frequently is essential for more than just their physical health. The daily walk also offers him some mental stimulation and quality bonding time with his/her human.

This breed is also capable of extreme loyalty to his/her human, establishing a life-long bond that is virtually impossible to break. They will love you unconditionally and want to do what they believe pleases you the most.

When a Lab forms a close bond with his/her human, he/she will ponder countless ways of trying and get his/her human's attention, whether good or bad. This means he/she will yank laundry from the line or basket, dig holes in your yard, or chew your shoes if he/she fells that's the only way you will center your attention back on him/her.

Although this type of negative behavior can become present in any breed, with a dog of high intellect and a solid sense of family bonding, it is even more significant to find ways to re-direct this behavior into positive behavior while your dog is still young.

Labrador Retrievers yearn for companionship. As far as they are concerned, you and your family are his/her pack. A Lab will not make a good kennel dog and will not react well to being left out alone in your backyard for long hours. In fact, they are more likely to undergo separation anxiety than other dogs if not trained early on how to deal with you leaving for work or elsewhere.

Having said that, if you do not have the time or patience to give to a Labrador Retriever with the training, exercise and companionship it craves, then think through looking into a different breed of dog.

Chapter 2: How Much Is Enough Exercise?

It's sad to hear people say "My dog doesn't really require that much exercise. He/she is happy to lie around all day."

Your dog lying around all day is never a good reason to assume that they don't require mental and physical exercise, particularly with a working breed such as the Labrador Retriever.

It is a fact that many Labrador Retriever dogs are happy and content when they are permitted to curl up anywhere near their owner and stay there for hours. But, they must also get the necessary physical exercise aside from cuddling.

A Labrador Retriever will be happy to be included in anything you are doing, but it simply is not enough for his physical health and well-being.

Walking

Your Lab will not think of going out for a walk as "exercise". He/she sees it as being invited by the family pack for a "hunt". He/she knows that they will have the chance to search for potential food, sniff around for other dogs or possible prey, and also spend quality time as part of the pack. For your Lab, this constitutes mental stimulation also.

Labrador Retrievers will naturally travel in a cantering-lope as opposed to a slow walk. While you are walking together, make sure you move at a brisk pace so that he/she is able to trot beside you in a contented step for his/her size. This might mean walking fast or maybe even jogging to ensure that you stay at the speed of his/her gait without him/her demanding to pull ahead.

In addition, walking is awesome for keeping knee, hip and elbow joints agile because Lab's are a larger breed. A lot of large breeds are well-known to suffer with hip complications later in life, thus regular exercise will help in keeping your adored dog fit and healthy for much longer.

Play Time

Lab's are instinctually full of life, inquisitive and curious. A bored Lab can swiftly become destructive when he/she is looking for something to occupy their mind. This can come in the form of digging in the garden, tearing laundry off the line, chewing your favorite shoes or just simply barking or crying out of pure boredom.

Play time is all about offering him/her a little time to just be silly and have some fun. Play time is also an essential time to strengthen the bond between you and your Lab.

Play time is also an important amount of your dog's exercise routine and should be such that your Lab finds it enjoyable and entertaining. You can teach your Lab to fetch a ball or Frisbee, and then throw it around for him/her in your yard or at the park. Most Labs enjoy playing tug-o-war. Find an appropriate rope toy and encourage him/her to play. This helps in strengthening their shoulder and jaw muscles.

You can also include games which will stimulate his/her mind and his/her desire to hunt, like hide-and-seek. Labs love to track down their human who is hiding in the closet, behind a bush, round the side of the house or behind a door. Make it a fun game, and applaud and praise him/her when he/she finds you.

<u>Hunting</u>

While Labs love to spend time hunting and tracking, this **doesn't** mean you need to take your Lab out to kill wild animals. You can always give him something in your own yard to track and hunt. It will be rewarding for him/her mentally and physically.

Try sprinkling a handful of biscuits around the yard and telling him/her to go and find them. He/she will spend as long as needed, sniffing every one of them out and have a great time doing it.

A lot of dog owners use specially made, non-toxic chew toys intended to hold treats inside. Your dog will thankfully spend time attempting get the food out. Just remember not to use sticky or wet food. This could attract ants.

The above games can teach your Lab to hunt down food and track hidden treats you have left around.

Chapter 3: Choosing Your Labrador Retriever Puppy

Labrador Retriever puppies are sweet, soft and so extremely irresistible. It is easy to see why so many individuals decide on these beautiful pups as pets.

Having said that, if you are intending to breed or show your Lab, always remember how important it is to select a reputable breeder who will be more than willing to give you the thorough family lineage and registration papers. This will assist you in determining the size, coat length, coloring and sometimes the temperament that the litter is expected to show as main features.

When getting a purebred Labrador Retriever, you should also inquire about medical histories of both the sire and the dam. This is because this breed can sometimes have genetic medical and psychological issues to watch out for.

These issues can consist of heart problems, hip or joint dysplasia, arthritis, higher risk of the potentially fatal "canine bloat" (gastric dilatation or gastric digestive volvulus syndrome), and other severe inherited problems.

What a lot of people tend to forget is that these endearing puppies will grow into big, powerful dogs quickly. You may well be dealing with an 80 pound dog with the attention and behavior of a bouncy, playful puppy.

This is the point where a lot of unprepared owners give up on their Lab. Some will give away the mischievous pup or even leave him/her at a shelter instead of taking the needed time to train them correctly to develop into the devoted, adoring, intelligent dog they have the potential to become.

For the best outcome, you should start basic training the instant your new puppy comes home.

Lab puppies are so amazingly smart. They will pick up on the simplest commands very fast, and if you remember to work together with them in a language they comprehend, it is very possible to teach your Lab puppy how to adjust his/her own behavior in order to suit the family pack rules, even while he/she is still very young.

The fundamentals to training such clever breeds of dog is to have sufficient patience and learn to use the praise-and- reward technique. This is expressly true with Labrador Retrievers, who respond very well to approval.

Your Lab will grow a robust sense of respect for you when you spend time teaching him/her, training him/her and disciplining him/her, to the point where he/she will happily do as you say purely because he/she knows it pleases you, which, in turn, pleases him/her.

You are also going to learn that such high levels of intelligence sometimes also comes with similarly high levels of stubbornness. This instinctively want to dominate. In dogs, domination is not about anger or violence. To them, it is about attempting to establish the pack order. And, your puppy will try eagerly to figure out where his position is in your family pack.

Chapter 4: Bringing Your Lab Puppy Home

Bringing your Lab puppy home for the first time will be an extremely exciting day for you, but it can be a nerve-wracking, frightening day for your new puppy. Think about it, he/she has had the comfort and company of 5 or 6 other litter-mates, and his/her mother since the day he/she was born. Now what he/she has is an unfamiliar brand new pack.

Your puppy may enjoy play time greatly when he/she first arrives, however the instant he/she is left on his/her own, the unexpected isolation will remind him/her that his/her mother is absent and that he/she has no litter-mates to snuggle up to for warmth and security.

A conscientious owner will afford their new puppy some place safe and comforting for their new puppy to sleep and also may offer him/her another litter-mate to help him/her feel safe. One of the best ways to do this is to either purchase or create a comfy bed and give him/her a stuffed toy that is just a bit larger than he/she is.

That stuffed toy may begin as a replacement litter-mate, but will more than likely wind up being your puppy's friend and play-mate as he/she grows. Puppy training should start on the first day home. This is where you institute the rules for what is suitable behavior and what is not. Potty training needs to be a priority right from the start.

Even though your puppy is tiny and cute initially, he/she will grow into a big dog, so, cuteness aside, it is not wise to encourage jumping, biting or getting onto your furniture at any time. You also should never give the puppy anything of your own to either play with or chew. Always make available toys and bedding of their own and spend time teaching him/her to pursue his/her own things rather than yours.

Always keep in mind that you should stop any puppy behavior that you don't want to see in your adult dog. By doing this, your Labrador Retriever will grow up comprehending what belongs to him/her and what belongs to you. He/she will also have a strong respect for the family/home rules early on and will show that respect.

Chapter 5: Speaking Your Dog's Language

A responsible Lab owner will always take the needed time to learn how to communicate successfully with their dog. In other words, learn to speak in a language the dog will understand.

When you provide a dog with a command or talk to him/her, he/she does not in fact listen to the words you are saying, but rather, your dog is reacting to the tone of your voice and position of your body or hand signal.

If you really take the time to listen to your dog, you will notice that he/she has an assortment of different barks at different levels, for warning, happy, greeting, growling, whining, whimpers, playful yips, attention-seeking and excitable or frisky barks. Each one of these barks is tone-based and has a variation of lengths and meanings.

If you want to encourage the dog to continue an acceptable behavior, you should praise him/her by means of a high-pitched, cheerful voice. You can even use a loving pat or small food reward if you are expressly happy with something he/she has done correctly. This will reinforce that what he/she has done is good and that you are very pleased.

On the other hand, if he/she is behaving badly or doing something that is unacceptable, give a quick reprimand which sounds a bit like a growl, like "ah ah". This will remind him/her of the throaty growls his/her mother would make to discipline him/her with when he/she was badly behaved. He/she will soon quit doing whatever earned him/her the reprimand.

Yelling at your Lab will never be seen as scolding them in their language. The dog will only assume that you are sending out similar warning barks as he/she does, or he/she will assume that you are being aggressive due to some threat that he/she cannot identify. When you yell at your dog, you risk making him/her nervous. However, you really will not be successfully disciplining him/her in any way. Yelling could make the behavior even worse.

A comforting tone of voice is good when your dog is having an affectionate moment with you, but giving the same comfort during a stressful or fearful time will not help your dog feel better.

As a matter of fact, if you reassure a dog when he is fearful, like in the middle of a thunderstorm, he might construe the comforting words as being right to be scared.

Giving your dog a treat just simply for being cute will give him/her the impression that he/she does not have to obey your orders to get treats. He/she will believe that if they wait long enough, you will give them something anyway.

In addition, you should differentiate between bribery and reward. Your Lab should get a treat after he/she has done something to earn it. The dog should not have to be shown a reward or be bribed into obeying the rules by waving a treat in front of its nose.

Always pay attention to how your dog is hearing the tone of your voice when you are training, scolding, or playing. Always keep in mind that rewards should be earned. If you follow this technique, you will notice that soon enough your dog will understand what is expected of him/her.

Chapter 6: Effective Discipline

Way too many people assume that the best way to discipline a dog is to whack his/her nose, yell at him/her, tie him/her up alone in the yard, or rub his/her nose in the mess he/she made.

To tell you the truth is, not one of these strategies work and is not effective discipline for any breed of dog. More than likely, you are actually making the dog's behavior even worse.

To effectively manage any form of discipline, it is essential to understand a bit about "dog language" and adapt your corrective methods to suit what your Lab will comprehend. Remember, a dog is most content when he/she can make his owner pleased.

Never hit a dog - not for any reason. Dogs view hitting as uncalled-for violent behavior. They do not understand why their human is lashing out and could, more than likely, develop an unhealthy fear of you. That fear may well leave your dog depressed, full of anxiety, violent behavior or other psychological problems. This is because your dog cannot figure out why you are violent toward him/her when all he/she really wanted to do was play.

Keep this in mind: An adult Lab has very sharp teeth and powerful jaws which could very effortlessly crush every bone in your hand or leg. You dog just simply chooses not to. Why? Because he/she possesses an unconditional love for you, irrespective of how he/she is being treated. Don't let them down.

By now, if you have discovered how to express your pleasure with your dog's positive actions, then you probably know that your dog constantly desires your approval, attention and affection. When you want to show him/her that you are not pleased with something, just ignore him/her for a few minutes. You can turn your back, folding your arms around your chest and looking the other way. To a dog, this is the worst of reprimands.

When your dog adjusts his/her behavior positively, excessively praise him/her with a cheerful, high-pitched tone. Feel free to also give your do a pat and say "good dog". He/she will learn very fast that he/she makes you happy when behaving well and will receive nothing when acting badly.

Here is another example of modifying bad behavior into good: Let's say you catch your dog chewing something they shouldn't be. Take away the item and give him a quick, stern "ah ah", and then substitute it with one of his/her toys. Then, praise your dog for playing with his own toy. You will be surprised how quickly they learn.

Chapter 7: Potty Training

Potty training your Lab puppy should be fairly easy. With a bit of patience, it should only take a couple days to teach your puppy to realize that he/she needs to relieve themselves outside.

If you use your increasing knowledge to teach your puppy what is expected of them, you will need even need to be concerned with a crate, puppy pads, newspaper or other anything else. Your dog is intelligent and can figure out quickly what is expected of them, but only if you do it correctly.

The initial step is to form a routine where you take your puppy outside at consistent intervals. They should be instantly after he/she wakes up from a nap, right after eating, more than a few times during the course of the day and prior to going to bed.

When outside, allow the puppy to roam around the yard a bit. Do not say anything. Do not play. Simply wait patiently. As soon as you notice your puppy getting into position to relieve themselves, say the command of your choosing, such as "go potty" or "do your pee pee". Repeat the command while your dog is peeing.
When finished, praise your dog with an affectionate pat and tell him/her "good dog".

Now, you will need to have a little patience. Of course, a puppy who thinks they are going to be praised for going to the bathroom will most likely try to get your attention by doing it again. The next time he/she feels the urge to go, they will make sure they do it right in front of you. However, that could be on the rug or somewhere in the house.

It is very important not to yell at or scold the dog for doing this. In its place, pick the dog up silently and take him/her outside to complete what he/she was doing. When you get out there, reinforce the command your chose like "go potty", and then be sure to give praise for attempting it again, but outside in the yard this time. Go back in the house and silently clean up the mess. Do not make eye contact. Do not make a fuss. Simply clean it up.

After just a few days of this, the puppy will start attempting to get your attention to go potty. You need to make sure you stay aware of the tactics your dog will try to get your attention. He/she may pull at your hand or your clothing with his/her teeth. He/she may whine or bark. He/she may attempt to get you to follow to the door by pawing. Regardless of what tactic your dog uses, be sure to let them outside every time until the routine is down pat. Praise your dog for going on their own and potty training will be complete before you know it.

Chapter 8: Basic Obedience Training

Spending lots of time training any breeds of dog is important, however Labs really thrive on the task of learning new things and making their human happy.

Because they are such intelligent dogs, you will likely learn that they are extremely easy to train. They really catch on fast as to what is anticipated of them. If you are willing to take the time to learn how to communicate successfully with your Lab, then it will be that much easier to teach him/her to become a happy, well-mannered member of your family.

Always provide a positive reward system when training. Offer dog a form of reward, such as a treat, for good behavior or doing something you want.

Sit

Sitting is a natural position, so it is so easy to teach him/her to sit. Take and hold a treat right above his/her nose. He/she should spontaneously in order to tilt his/her head back enough to get a better view and sniff at the treat.

The instant the dog's bottom hits the ground, say the command "sit". Then give him/her the treat and say "good dog" or "good sit". You can also give him/her an affectionate pat to emphasize the reward.

After a few times doing this command, your dog will comprehend that the command "sit" means he/she is most likely going to receive a reward and a pat if he/she sits.

When your dog begins to understand this simple command you provide, you can then start to present more training commands. Now the dog already understands that he/she will be rewarded when they do what you want, so they will instantly attempt to do what makes you happy and what he/she knows will get him/her a treat and more affection.

Drop

Teaching your Lab to lie down on his stomach on command can be beneficial. It is also an easy command to teach, because it is a natural position for your dog.
Once again, start by holding the reward above his/her nose and telling your dog to sit. When he/she sits, they will already be expecting a treat. However, do not give it to him/her yet. Instead, bring the reward down towards his/her front feet and move it somewhat forward. This move will encourage the dog to lower his/her head to reach for the treat.

Lightly encourage the dog to drop down into a lying position on his/her stomach by providing a gentle nudge on the dog's shoulders. Do not ever push or force the dog into position. When the dog does lay down, say "drop" and provide the dog with the treat.

Repeat this command a few times a day until your dog starts happily dropping on command.

Come

Before you are able to permit your dog to go anywhere with you without a leash on, it is extremely important to teach him/her to come to you when called. This is termed a "recall". As you know, Labs are large dogs. While to you your dog is harmless, strangers do not know your pet and might become frightened or angry at an unrestrained dog jumping all over them.

Your dog must understand that when you call him/her, it will amount to rewards and attention. The dog will not want to return to you if he/she believes that you are going to yell at or scold him/her, or punish him/her in any way.

Start by taking the dog to the park on a long leash. If you have already trained the dog to heel while walking, then provide him/her a release command which will tell him/her that it is okay to roam around without the need to heel. (If not, there is a more detailed chapter on Leash Training later in this book).

When your dog's attention is no longer on you, say in a high-pitched, happy voice "come". Open your arms wide, but do not bend down to the dog's level. Continue standing.

If he/she comes to you immediately, praise him/her and provide a treat for returning when called. But, if the dog ignores you, give his/her leash a mild tug and repeat the command again until he/she obeys. When he/she reaches your feet, encourage him/her to sit before you give the reward.

The praise and reward part of this command are very important, so your dog will understand that it is worth it to come back when called. Repeat this command a few times during your walks and gradually lengthen the distance you allow your dog to wander before calling him/her back.

Fetch

Not all dogs will fetch a ball or stick automatically. Some dogs require encouragement to learn how to play this way. However, once your dog learns this exercise, it will become lots of fun for dog and for you.

A tennis ball is typically a good way to start teaching your dog to fetch. Roll the ball on the ground and cheer the dog on to chase it. As he/she reaches the ball, say "fetch". Once that dog has picked it up, praise him/her lots and give lots of affection. Your dog will learns quickly that picking up the ball will bring attention from you.

When he/she is comfortable chasing the ball and picking it up, hold off on giving the reward now. Instead, call the dog to you and encourage him/her to return to you while still holding the ball. When he/she gets back to you, praise him/her for bringing it back.

Stay

Teaching your Lab to stay for any reason can be a helpful command. You may want the dog to sit and stay in another room away from the front door while you answer it, or to teach him/her to leave his/her food bowl alone until he/she is told that it is okay to eat it, or maybe just to get him/her to understand not to leave the yard. There are so many reasons the "stay" command can be useful.

It is, however, a little harder to teach your dog to stay, as you will be rewarding him/her for doing nothing at all. Many dogs are naturally disposed to follow you around, so they will not instantly comprehend why you would give him a treat for sitting and doing nothing.

Hold a treat above his/her nose and tell your dog to sit. When he/she is sitting, the dog will be waiting for a treat. Do not provide it yet.

In a firm voice, say "stay". Raise your hand, palm out, fingers together, like a stop sign.

Take one step backward, away from the dog. Repeat the command "stay". You want your dog to remain sitting until you tell him/her otherwise. Wait 2 or 3 seconds and repeat the command and the hand signal, and then step back towards him/her again.

If your dog remained in position, give him/her the treat and praise. Steadily increase the distance and the time you wait to return until your dog comprehends that you want him/her to simply sit around and do nothing until you get back with the reward.

Ultimately, your dog will understand that he/she will get positive attention, praise and affection if he/she just stays put when told. You will eventually even be able to leave your dog's direct line of sight and be confident that he/she will be sitting there when you return.

Never call the dog to you after you have asked him/her to stay. Rather, always return to him/her to release him/her from the command.

Wait

Teaching your dog to "wait" is not the same as "stay". It can also be a bit more difficult for the dog to comprehend the difference between the 2 commands. The dog is still expected to stay in the same spot. But, the difference between "wait" and "stay" is very important.

The "wait" command is very important if you aim to continue your dog's training past the basics, and into agility work.

When you request your dog to wait, you want him/her to stay still until you call him/her to you.

Once your dog has successfully learned that "stay" means not to move, you should work on a different tone for the command to "wait".

Tell your dog to sit. Use a casual voice and say "wait" using a warning finger. The dog will notice the difference in your voice hand signal, but will not immediately know why. Walk a two or three steps away, and then give the command to "come". Be encouraging.

At first, the dog may be confused as to why he/she is allowed to move from the "stay" position. Strengthen this lesson by giving your dog a very firm-voiced "stay" with a stop-signal hand sign. Walk two or three steps away, and return before giving the reward.

Now use the casual tone for "wait" with one warning finger raised. The dog should still be sitting, so move a number of steps away before calling him/her back to you.

It is important to be very patient when teaching the subtle difference between these commands. Make sure you are consistent in your tone and expectation. Your dog will soon understand what you want.

# Chapter 9: Leash Training Your Lab

Have you ever noticed a person being dragged around behind their dog on a leash? It is pretty much as though the dog is taking the owner for a walk. Dogs who pull at the leash and drag their humans around usually have pack-leadership problems. They think that they are the one in control don not have a clear understanding of who the real leader of the pack is.

Having said that, an adult Lab can be extremely powerful. The last thing you need is a heavy-duty dog who you cannot control during a walk. Therefore, it is extremely important to start the leash training at a very young age.

Your dog has to understand when you want him to walk at "heel" (by your side), and when it is alright for him/her to roam a bit and sniff around. Prior to teaching that stage, however, you must first teach the dog that walking at "heel" is the correct location to be in unless you tell him/her otherwise.

The Correct Leash and Collar

Never buy a leash or collar that is too big for your dog. Because Lab puppies grow very quickly, you may need to purchase more than a few new collars as he/she is growing. Training, however, will be much easier given the correct size lease and collar are obtained.

Leash Training a Young Puppy

A lot of trainers support fastening a leash to your dog's collar in order to get him/her used to having it there for a short while every day for at least a week or so. This is good advice, but a Labrador Retriever is smart enough even at a young age to understand what the leash means immediately upon going out for the first walk.

Your puppy's first walk should be an aimless stroll around the yard or just a short distance along the street. Your aim is to teach your puppy that having a collar on and being attached to a leash means he/she will get to follow you around and see new things without anything bad happening to him/her. Initially, the dog will have no idea what is going on, so just take a few steps and inspire the dog to follow you.

You should never tug on the leash and do not allow it to get tight. Never drag your puppy or he could grow a fear of the collar and leash. Merely encourage him/her with your voice to follow you while you walk.

If the puppy decides the walk is exciting, as puppies do, and starts to run ahead, do not tug on the leash or pull the puppy back to you. Just encourage him/her to come back to you by calling.

You should never walk for too long with a very young puppy. The initial walks are just to five the puppy the idea that you are to see and smell new and exciting things, as long as he/she follows and listens. Praise your puppy when he/she sprints along loyally behind you.

Leash Training an Overexcited Puppy

Lab puppies are naturally inquisitive and playful. Once the puppy starts to comprehend that going for a walk is fun and exciting, he will naturally start to pull away. You might also notice that as he/she gets older, your dog will start testing your power and pack leadership a bit, which is sometimes also a reason for pulling ahead. This is where you begin serious leash-training methods.

The best way to reclaim control over a dog who is pulling away from you is to change direction abruptly. Do not yell at the dog or reprimand for pulling. Merely turn in the opposite direction and give the high-pitched, happy command "watching".

This lets your dog know that he/she is not in trouble, but should pay attention since you have changed direction. Your dog will look up and realize that you have switched directions. He will now most likely turn around to catch up with you.

When the dog catches up and is walking beside you, say "heel". Take a few steps and if your dog is still next to you, give praise.

Initially, your dog may not comprehend why you are praising for basically walking, so he/she will instantly try to pull away and walk in front of you again. Give a short, "ah ah", and change direction again, saying "watching" in a happy voice.

Again, the dog ought to run to catch up with you. Reiterate the command "heel" the instant he/she is walking at your side and praise when he/she remains there. The longer your dog remains at your side, continue giving encouraging words of praise.

Meeting Other Dogs and Other People

When you walk with your dog, you are very probably going to come across other people and dogs. A lot of dogs will bark/growl at forthcoming dogs. Some dogs will get so excited by the notion of meeting a new playmate that they will yip eagerly and start to pull at the leash to say hello.

Some dogs will even raise their spines threateningly. This is typically a warning sign for fear that the strange dog could pose a threat to you and/or him, thus the dog is exhibiting a warning to the other dog not to approach.

Because of this, your dog must be taught that these strange people and animals are not intimidating or dangerous to him or you.

Tell him/her to sit even before he/she sees the distraction. Praise him/her for being calm and wait beside him/her until the distraction approaches. As it gets closer, assure your dog with a happy voice. It does not even really matter what you say – your tone is what is important.

If the individuals appear anxious around a large, barking dog, give him/her words of encouragement which the people can hear. This will calm your dog, and also help to reassure the strangers. Say something such as "they are not scary people. You are a good dog. I know it is exciting, but sit down. Be a good boy/girl."

You are pretty much diffusing all the exciting parts of being near new people or strange dogs and distracting him/her long enough to realize that there is no threat involved. There was no playing or interacting involved. In fact, the whole encounter was quite boring. Your dog will learn quickly that there's no need to bark or growl or yip the next time.

Chapter 10: Socializing Your Labrador Retriever

Most Labs are very loyal to their "pack". When they have an understanding of who is part of that pack and what the pecking order is, they will consider themselves part of it.

Nevertheless, you might also discover that this pack instinct can decipher to a distrust of other people or dogs who they consider to be from "other packs".

Socializing the dog with other people and dogs is enormously important. Your dog must understand how to be good around strangers and unfamiliar dogs without becoming hostile or overly protective of you.

Be aware that socializing doesn't necessarily mean taking the dog for a playdate with every other dog in the neighborhood at the doggy park. This is a human concept and not familiar to most dogs. Not all dogs will be happy to socialize with strange dogs they view as being from an opposing pack.

Effective socializing means teaching your dog to be accustomed to meeting new people, and teaching him/her how to react when he/she meets new dogs.

The best way to present your Lab to a countless new dogs and people is to join in a puppy class. In a group class, the puppy will have the chance to associate with all kinds of new friends. This can help to teach him/her that dogs from "rival packs" are not a threat to him/her or you, and will help stop him/her from developing hostile behavior as he/she gets older.

Chapter 11: How to Stop Biting and Chewing

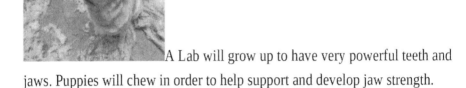A Lab will grow up to have very powerful teeth and jaws. Puppies will chew in order to help support and develop jaw strength.

Keep in mind that chewing is a natural behavior for a puppy, so attempting to stop it completely will not work. Yet, it is possible to redirect your dog's chewing into more positive areas.

This means teaching your dog what is acceptable to chew and what is not. This simple lesson will afford your dog the capability to chew when he needs to, without ruining your favorite shoes or furniture.

The best way to do this is to provide him with non-toxic chew toys. They can be rubber or rope – it doesn't really matter. Just be sure the toys are safe. Avoid small parts or sticks that could harm gums or internal organs. What is important is that your dog understands his toys are his own.

The next time you find your dog chewing on something that does not belong to him/her, do not scold. Instead, simply take the item silently and replace it with one of his/her own toys. Do not ever scold a dog for exhibiting a natural behavior.

When your dog picks up his own toy and focuses on it, praise him. Spend a little time playing with the toy with him/her so he/she understands the positive association of chewing his own toy.

After a little persistence, you'll soon find that any time your dog wants attention, or wants to play, or just wants to chew, he'll automatically pick up his own toys and leave your things alone.

Biting

If you spend some time observing a litter of puppies playing, you will see that they bite each other as part of their play. While this might look cute when they are young, as a Lab grows, his teeth and jaws become more powerful, and it is no longer fun.

Together with play-biting, some dogs also "mouth" their humans. This is essentially a display of affection in most cases, and an attempt to seek attention in others. Once again, this is considered inappropriate behavior in an adult dog, especially if you have guests or visitors over.

You will need to spend time showing your dog how to play-bite on a positive level. This is where his own non-toxic chew toys can become his way of showing you affection and seeking attention in a positive way.

When you notice your dog is mouthing you or biting at your hands or arms playfully give him a sharp "ah ah" and remove your hand. Then encourage him to grab his chew toy instead and spend some time playing with him to reinforce the positive connotations of biting an acceptable object rather than your hand.

Chapter 12: Advanced Training Techniques

Labrador Retrievers thrive on challenges. Their high intelligence level means they will delight in the notion of more difficult training tasks. This makes the Lab an excellent breed for trial and agility work. As long as they realize there's a reward, some fun and some praise in it for them at the end of the task, they will work hard to get it correct.

Identical principles of positive reward training apply with more advanced training techniques. The major difficulty is getting your dog to comprehend what is expected each exercise.

There are lots of advanced training you can work on with your dog which stems from the most basic lessons he/she learned as a puppy. You may want to train your dog to pick up his/her own toys and put them in a toy box when finished playing with them. You may want to have your dog fetch the newspaper for you every morning.

Or you may want to enroll him/her in an agility training course to help keep him/her active and stimulated.

It is important not to start agility training or any advanced training which involves jumping until after your dog is older than eighteen months. Young bones require time to strengthen and develop properly. This will help to avoid injuries that may affect your dog's health later in life.

You should also be sure your dog comprehends and obeys the basic commands to sit, drop, go left and right, wait and come to you when he/she is called.

Most dog training classes will have an obstacle course for agility work. If you are able to enroll in a dog class for basic training, you should be able to continue your dog's training into the more advanced classes.

You can always get your dog used to the hurdles and obstacles by building a small agility course at home in the yard. You can use a low bench as a hurdle and some cones placed around the yard as an obstacle course.

To start, command the dog to sit on one side of the hurdle. When he/she is sitting, tell him/her to wait and move around to the other side of the hurdle. Show him/her you have a treat or favorite toy of his/hers and call him/her to you, encouraging him/her to jump over the hurdle to get to you. As he/she jumps, say "over" or "jump" and praise him/her highly when he/she gets to you. Your dog will quickly get the idea that jumping over the hurdle means rewards.

Also, try throwing a ball over the hurdle and get him/her to fetch it. Initially, the dog will run around the hurdle to get the ball, but encourage him/her to jump over, and jump over it again as he/she brings it back. Your dog will quickly start to comprehend that it is a game and is fun – specifically if he/she getting plenty of positive attention.

Printed in Great Britain
by Amazon

35705356R00027